Magic

MW01294089

Defend Against Curses, Gossip, Bullies,
Thieves, Demonic Forces, Violence,
Threats and Psychic Attack

THE GALLERY OF
MAGICK

Damon Brand

CONTENTS

Why You Need Protection

There are many ways to protect yourself with magick. Some books show you how to defend against curses and psychic attack, but this book can also help to shield you from cruel people, bullies, bad luck, gossip and people who undermine you.

If you are afraid of violence, robbery or random accidents, you can help to make yourself safe with magick. If somebody is merely unpleasant, you can protect yourself from their subtle malice. If somebody means you great harm, you can stop them in their tracks.

You can protect yourself, your home, your work and your loved ones, all with a series of simple rituals.

You may think you are cursed or under psychic attack. If so, you can put an end to the attack. You may think you've done something wrong or performed 'bad magick' in the past. You may even believe that somebody has cast the 'evil eye' upon you. This book can take away such problems.

If you've never performed magick before, that is absolutely fine. Even if magick is new to you, everything you need to know to protect yourself is included in these pages. *Magickal Protection* is a great way to get into magick, but the book has also been written for people who are already deeply involved with magick. It should be perfect for beginners while giving advanced protection to experienced occultists.

8

How Much Protection You Need

If you are under attack from a bully, a cruel boss, a mean partner or an unknown assailant, you need protection. If you feel you are having a run of bad luck or that you may be cursed, you need protection. There are thousands of reasons why this book can work for you. It can keep you safe from strange psychic dangers, or protect you from something as ordinary and deadly as a random road accident.

It's important, though, to get some perspective. Life is not always safe, and that's actually OK. The easiest way to avoid danger is simply to lock yourself away, to avoid all harm. But that, of course, is no way to live.

When children are playing, we repeatedly tell them to 'be careful' or to stop hanging upside down off that tree branch, because we're afraid of the danger. And yet we still let them play. Those kids are having a great time, and it's worth risking a broken arm for the sake of experiencing an exciting life. But we don't want our kids to get hurt, so we protect them as well as we can; from people, from illness, from accidents.

Finding a good balance is the difficult part, and the same is true with magick. You may live an ordinary life and want protection. You may lead a magickal life and need supernatural protection. Or you may lead an adventurous life, or work in a dangerous career and need protection from the inherent dangers.

This book encourages you to protect yourself when needed, but I don't want you to spend your life living in fear and putting up all the barriers you can to ensure no harm will ever come to you. That approach merely shows that you are terrified of life, and then you will probably attract more bad luck. This book should give you sufficient protection that you can be courageous in the world, and experience everything you want to experience.

If you really, really want to avoid having an airplane crash, the obvious advice is - *don't fly airplanes*. But, clearly, that's not useful advice. If you love flying or need to fly for work, or just want to take a vacation, then you can use magick to make it as safe as possible. Anybody that wants to fly should fly.

That doesn't mean you won't ever crash. I am a trained private pilot, and I fly occasionally. I used to be a keen pilot, flying all the time, and even when using magickal protection I had some near misses, involving engine problems, other aircraft getting too close and unexpected bad weather. I survived, but not always without a scratch. I still feel grateful, though, because I managed to get out of situations that were potentially deadly. When you fly a lot – and I mean *a lot* - you tend to crash occasionally. To me, magick gave me the confidence to fly often, and get away with it even when the odds were against me.

I used protection magick to keep me safe while traveling through a city once, but I was robbed. Does this mean the magick was a failure? Not at all. They only took my credit cards, which I promptly canceled, and they never noticed the big wad of cash that was clearly visible in my wallet. Everything was back to normal in twenty-four hours, and I was barely shaken. I can only think that the magick made that robbery as bearable as it could have been.

The point of these stories is to show that protection magick will help keep you safe, but it will not shield you entirely from life, and nor should it aim to do so. Life is an adventure, and we sometimes have accidents and problems.

This book is aimed at protecting you from the sort of unpleasantness that makes life feel unfair, unkind and unbearable. There are times when you have bad luck, feel afraid of people, get pushed around, get cursed or attacked by people, and this magick can put a stop to that. You can also protect yourself from accidents as well as protecting your home and family.

I only tell the two stories above – about the flying and the robbery – to be as honest as possible, and say that although you will be genuinely shielded, you won't be invincible. You must still take care and look after yourself.

I have often used ritual magick to remain 'invisible' in dangerous areas because I enjoy passing through such places, but I also know that it's important to keep a low profile. When passing through those areas, I don't attract attention to myself. *You need to contribute to the magick.* If your home is under threat from thieves, get good locks as well as good magick.

This might sound outrageously obvious, but many people think that magick will be so powerful they can do whatever they want and remain protected. A young man I knew used a protection ritual to avoid violence, and went out on a drunken night, believing he could verbally abuse anybody he wanted. He found out how wrong he was. Mind you, when he was punched, he did manage to keep his teeth intact, so perhaps the magick helped after all. The point here is that protection magick is meant to keep you safe, not to make you a superhero.

If you're actually under the threat of violence from a known person, your first job is to report that person to the police. If you are in a domestic situation where you are afraid of somebody, you can use magick to subdue that person for a while, but you need to plan a way out of that situation and seek help and support from others. This is common sense, but it is often difficult to see when you are stuck in that situation.

The magick in this book is simple to set up and use and can make your life much calmer and safer, clear away past problems and prevent you from being hurt. Follow the instructions confidently, and you will get results.

The Sense of Danger

This book aims to protect you from real-world danger, such as robbery and car accidents, but it is also aimed at stopping curses, hexes, psychic attacks and crossed conditions.

Crossed conditions can occur when you are on the wrong spiritual path (through chasing dreams that aren't really your own,) when you have inadvertently offended a spirit through substandard magick, spent time in a place that is sacred to others, or passed through a place that is tainted with evil. You can also be crossed if somebody hates you powerfully enough, even if they have no occult experience. The same crossed conditions can arise from the repetition of negative comments about yourself to yourself.

A man wrote to me recently and said he was doing all the magick he could think of but then added, 'I try and try and try and never get any reward.' What a powerful spell *that* was. He was cursing himself with that negative statement. I pointed that out to him, and he replied by saying, 'I'm always making mistakes like that.' That's another powerful spell, directed straight at *himself*. This is not to say you need to go around being a positive thinker, but it is possible that negative thoughts can accumulate to the point of leaving you blocked from further spiritual or material progression.

How do you know that you've been cursed, attacked or crossed? Generally, you don't, unless somebody has told you that they're cursing you. The symptoms of any psychic attack or curse are all quite similar and can be identical to the feeling of crossed conditions.

The symptoms include a general feeling of disconnection from the world and from people, a sense of depression, bad luck and a series of accidents and minor annoyances, nightmares, a sense of dread, or the feeling of being watched. You may have continual illnesses, repeated computer problems (such as lost passwords), a feeling of being vague, with a fuzzy-headed sense of self, tiredness, with a poor memory, while generally feeling low and sad for no reason.

You may also feel disliked, and that life is pointless. You may feel afraid for no discernible reason, and you may even experience physical phenomena such as noises, flashes of light or glimpses of entities out of the corner of your eye. Sometimes these phenomena escalate slowly over the years, so gradually that you almost think of them as normal. Sometimes they start so suddenly that you can be certain that you're under attack.

Of course, these symptoms could be caused by everyday challenges or mental problems – and you should always check on those first - but if in doubt, there is no harm in getting the magick started to protect yourself. Everybody feels the above symptoms from time to time, but you can be fairly certain that you've been cursed or crossed if four or more of these symptoms occur on a regular basis. You may also just get an intuition that you've been attacked. Trust that intuition.

Does it matter where the attack comes from? Not really, because although you may be *certain* an ex-spouse is likely to have cursed you, you could be wrong, and then you might end up expending a lot of magickal energy on the wrong person.

Most of the magick in this book is designed simply to protect you, rather than finding out who might be attacking you. Trying to find out the source of an attack can be draining. Also, one of the first protections people use when cursing is to ensure that they remain anonymous. If it's a well-designed curse, that can lead to you becoming paranoid when you try to discover the source of the curse, and you'll end up suspecting everybody.

It's best not to worry about how you were cursed, attacked or crossed, and instead, simply protect yourself.

There are rituals that can stop specific bullies and enemies in this book, and then you *do* need to know who is attacking you in order to stop them. The details required for those rituals will be explained when you come to them.

There was a time when I was repeatedly attacked, in a highly vicious manner, by somebody (or a group of people)

14

who used every tactic imaginable to keep me cursed. Every time I stopped the curse, they tried a new way to get to me. None of it mattered. I simply used the magick in this book. Every time I did so, they were stopped and eventually they gave up.

You are unlikely to be the subject of such a major attack, so be assured that you can uncross yourself, or stop curses with this magick, and it won't take much time or effort at all.

How to Use this Book

You can use this book any way you like, but to get the most out of it, do the following:

1. Learn *The Sword Banishing* and practice it twice a day as instructed, every day.

2. Perform the *Master Protection Ritual* for thirty-three days. (In the future, if you ever feel you are subject to an attack or a run of bad luck, repeat this *Master Protection Ritual* for another thirty-three days. It's unlikely you'll need to do this more than once every few years. The ritual protects you against bad luck, violence, random accidents and shields you from curses and psychic attack. It is the core of the book and is hugely powerful.)

3. Use the Protection Rituals that make up the rest of the book at any time, to solve particular problems or set up specific defenses, but please note that they will work better when you have spent a few days using *The Sword Banishing* and the *Master Protection Ritual*.

If you need to use a specific ritual right away, go ahead, but learn *The Sword Banishing* and *Master Protection Ritual* as soon as you can. With that said, there are several ways you may want to approach this.

Scenario 1: General Protection

You just want to learn about protection and put up some defenses. Learn *The Sword Banishing* and after a few days, when you feel you're getting to grips with it, start learning the *Master Protection Ritual* as well. Use the Protection Rituals if you ever need them.

Scenario 2: You're Concerned About a Possible Attack

If you feel you *may* be under some sort of psychic attack or that your luck is particularly bad, begin with *The Sword Banishing* and *Master Protection Ritual* on the same day. If there's no improvement within a few days, look at Scenario 3.

Scenario 3: You're Under Attack and Need Urgent Help

Let's say you know you've been cursed, or your house is the target of thieves, or a bully is making your life hell – you know something is wrong, and you want it stopped. Go straight to the best Protection Ritual for your needs and carry it out immediately. This will bring you some relief.

Then learn *The Sword Banishing* and *The Master Protection Ritual* as soon as possible – ideally you should begin working with them on the same day. This is quite a lot of magickal work at one time, but if you're desperate to get to the Protection Rituals, it's best to put up as much protection as possible.

You can perform more than one Protection Ritual at a time if you have the energy, but often there is no need. If you find the *right* ritual and direct it at the *source* of your problem, you may not need to use five or six rituals. However, in an extreme emergency, it is quite possible to combine five or six rituals to ensure that an enemy is stopped and that you remain safe. This will take time and energy, so only use multiple rituals if you really require them. It's better to spend ten minutes really working out what protection you need than to spend an hour every day doing six rituals that might not be required.

Please note that all rituals take several days. If you miss a day, it's not going to ruin the ritual, but it can weaken the results, so carry on with the ritual as soon as you are able, and continue working until you've performed it for the required number of days. So, if a ritual lasts for three days, make sure you perform it on three different days, even if it takes you a month to do so. Ideally, of course, you should work three days in a row, but that isn't always possible.

Although each ritual takes several days, none of them are too time-consuming, and they can be carried out in private without the need for any equipment such as candles, oils, chalk circles or wands. This should make it easy for you to get started.

What Happens When You Banish?

A banishing serves several purposes. At its most basic, a banishing ritual offers protection. It's a way of saying 'go away' quite forcefully to anything supernatural that may be nearby. It clears a psychic space around yourself and puts up a protective barrier. This is an ideal way to prepare your space before working any magick as it ensures there are no unwanted presences that might latch onto your psychic energy.

If that's the case, why haven't I published a banishing in my previous books? The books published to date have contained in-built constraints and protection, along with major behind-the-scenes magick that we have employed to ensure that the workings are safe. If you're using books such as *Words of Power, Magickal Cashbook* or *The 72 Angels of Magick,* you don't need to banish, but it's optional, and many people find it enhances the overall process. If, however, you choose to work with the darker side of magick, you may find that access to a banishing ritual can be comforting and useful. Whatever magick you use, it can help.

The main reason to use a daily banishing, however, is for the general protection it provides, as well as improving your magickal focus.

Many people have asked me to share the banishing ritual used by The Gallery of Magick, because they are afraid of a supernatural presence or curse, and feel the need to protect themselves. Violence and attacks of all kinds happen frequently, and people have asked me for help, so this feels like the right time to make this banishing available.

If you have been cursed or attacked psychically, banishing rituals can limit the effects of the attack so you can start using the ritual right away. You will need to deal with the attack separately as well, and that will be explained later in the book. Get started with banishing as soon as you can. It won't solve all your problems by itself, but it will limit any attacks on you and prepare you for other protection rituals. And then when you have solved all your problems, a twice-daily banishing can protect you from future attacks of all kinds.

The banishing should be practiced twice a day. Given that the entire banishing can be performed mentally, this is easy to do. If you practice this banishing twice every day, you are much less likely to be the victim of any type of psychic attack or curse.

You are not obliged to banish every day, and sometimes I feel so at ease with the world that I don't bother to banish. But if you want to keep up the best protection, a banishing performed twice each day, is a good way to sharpen your magickal powers and protect yourself.

You are free to learn any banishing you like, and there are many on offer (free of charge, online), but this book reveals *The Sword Banishing*, which was developed by The Gallery of Magick between 1982 and 1988. It was further refined in more recent years, and it is the one we prefer to use.

The beauty of this banishing is that it can be performed in silence, using nothing more than your imagination. Many styles of banishing involve wandering around in circles, waving daggers and shouting out angelic names, which can be a surprisingly enjoyable and dramatic experience, but it isn't ideal if you want to perform magick quickly and discreetly.

Some people like to banish as soon as they finish a ritual, to make sure that whatever spirit they called upon has gone off to do its work. I don't usually banish after a ritual because it seems like overkill. If you've asked the spirit to go and do its work, it should leave without being forced to leave.

Imagine asking an employee to come closer so you can whisper something, telling your worker what task you want them to do next, and then you push them away roughly to make sure they get on with the job. If you banish at the end of a ritual, it can feel a bit like that, or at least like you are slamming the door on your guest. So as a rule, I give a spirit license to depart, leave it at that, and use banishing separately.

I *will* banish after a ritual if the spirit seems to linger in my mind, or if there are unexpected side effects, such as crashes, bangs and so on. If anything feels a bit too supernatural or outside of my control, then I will banish to shut it up.

Crashes and bangs aren't usually anything to worry about. Often it can just be a sign that the spirit is connected to you harmlessly, but it can sometimes mean that something else slipped in during the ritual and is trying to cause mischief. And if you've called on a particularly aggressive demon that refuses to leave, you might want to shut it up so you can get on with your day. If anything's disturbing you, you have the right to banish it and find some peace.

Of course, crashes and bangs can just be paranoia. If you keep a log of how many times a bird flies into your window or a cat screeches, or you get sick – it happens all the time. But when it occurs after a ritual, people often assume the worst and think they're under attack. If in doubt, you can banish. It's quick and easy, and it works, but there's no need to banish after every single magickal act.

A banishing doesn't just say 'go away.' It also has the slightly ironic effect of making you more visible on the astral plane – that is, you become more noticeable to all supernatural entities. A good banishing makes you visible while offering protection so that only the spirits you directly and deliberately want to contact will get through to you.

This is why I like to banish *before* a ritual. It clears the space, it makes sure I'm visible to any being I may call, and it strengthens my psychic power. I know that after a banishing I am shining brightly on the astral plane and that making contact with spirits of all kinds will be safer and easier.

Whatever banishing you use, this psychic brightness can make you attractive to unwanted entities. The vast majority of the time they will not be able to do anything other than make a noise, make your mood change, or alter the atmosphere in the room slightly. If you complete a ritual and feel any sense of unease, or that an unwanted entity has been attracted into your life feel free to banish again, and you will be safe.

You can reserve banishing for rituals, or make it a regular part of your daily magickal work to keep you safe. Personally,

I banish twice a day (as described in the following paragraph) and will banish again any time that I am about to perform a magick ritual. This is the approach that I recommend.

It's ideal to banish twice a day, once in the morning and once at night. This will make yourself more receptive to magickal results, and safe from curses, attacks and physical harm. If you want to work on your magickal development, this is a routine that you should employ.

If you cannot banish twice a day, don't worry. You won't suddenly be assailed by hordes of demons. But if you can find the time to make this a regular practice, it only takes moments, and the benefits are noticeable.

In an ideal world, you should perform the first banishing before sunrise and the second banishing after sunset. Not many of us live in an ideal world. You may work shifts, have kids, have to get up when the alarm goes off, or just be too busy to get this work done. There are many things that make the ideal approach impossible. If that's the case, don't worry, but perform the banishing when you can.

I've found the most useful time to do the banishing is as soon as I awaken, before getting up. Where I live (most of the time), that's before sunrise. If the sun has risen, I don't worry about it and banish anyway.

Doing the banishing in bed, before you get up, only works if you can wake up without disturbing anybody because if you have kids or a partner, you don't want them talking while you're performing magick.

I perform the second banishing just before falling asleep. So it's always performed in bed, with my eyes closed, when I appear to be going to sleep.

I know people who perform the banishing while in the shower (it wastes water, but offers privacy), or when pretending to visit the bathroom. It's not glamorous, but angels really don't mind where you are or what you're doing when you banish.

Some people do the banishing when being driven to work (but this requires the luxury of having a driver – you don't want to do any magick while you're driving your own car), or while sitting on a train. There are many times to get this banishing done once you make the commitment.

The good news is that you don't need an altar or robe or any purification rituals. There's no need for candles, salt, herbs, oils or incense. Despite this, our simple banishing works as effectively as any we've known when you follow the instructions as written.

The Sword Banishing that follows is simple to execute and calls on angels that are easy to access. Direct contact with angels is fundamental to quick success with a banishing. I have used banishings that didn't work for several months because it took so long to contact the mighty entities I was calling on.

Our banishing has been developed to be as effective as any other, but it employs angels that can be contacted with nothing more than the mention of their names and a simple magickal thought.

A Note on Pronunciation

Read the words that are in capital letters as though they are written in English.

When you see the spirit name Alphun, it is actually pronounced AL-FUN. After each spirit name or word of power, the pronunciation will be written in capitals, something like this:

Alphun (AL-FUN)

In this example, AL would sound like *pal* without the *p*, and FUN is just the word *fun*. So Alphun is pronounced AL-FUN. This makes it extremely easy to pronounce everything you need.

The only sound that presents a challenge is CH as in the angelic name Yohach. This would be written as YO-HACH, but the CH is not the sound you find in *choose*. If you know the Scottish word Lo**ch** or the German word A**ch**tung, that's the CH sound you're aiming for.

If you feel the need for further guidance, there is an audio/video guide on The Gallery of Magick website (**www.galleryofmagick.com**), and that will make the whole process much easier for you.

If you simply can't get that CH to sound right (and that does happen with some people due to their accent and dialect), then simply use the K sound when you see CH. So, for Yohach, you would say YO-HAK. This is not ideal, but it will still work.

People worry about getting the pronunciation right more than just about anything else in magick, but it is not all that important. Nothing is worse for your magick than *worrying* about getting it precisely correct. It's better to do magick often, with bold intent and confidence than to aim for perfection.

You can trust that these pronunciations have been tested on many people, and they work.

More detailed pronunciation will be provided for every word at the end of the book, to ensure that you feel confident, but be assured that the system has been developed with visual sigils to ensure that it is Pronunciation Proof. Only use the pronunciation guide if you actually get stuck.

The Sword Banishing

The Sword Banishing calls on the powers of the angels Yohach, Kalach, Natzariel and Oziel. The activation, which sets this ritual up for you, also uses seven divine names, making a total of eleven names.

You will need to learn how to say these eleven names to activate the banishing, but you will use only the *four* angel names on a daily basis.

If this seems like a difficult task, please be aware that many banishings require you to learn countless movements, gestures, words, calls, and visualizations. Some require daggers, swords, chants, chalk circles, incense, and other paraphernalia. This banishing is about as simple as it gets but no less powerful. The banishing can last you a lifetime, so if you're serious about protection, take the time to learn the eleven names.

First, get used to saying the following eleven names out loud. Later you will be able to say the *four* angelic names silently, in your mind, but for now, learn what they sound like and feel like when you say them.

Pronunciation is *not* a big deal, so if you see the names and feel confident saying them, go ahead. I have received hundreds and hundreds of messages about pronunciation, so there is a pronunciation glossary at the back of the book for every word used here if you need it, but the main message is: don't worry about pronunciation! If you do worry, use the video on the website to guide you.

Here is the list of eleven names.

YOHACH
KALACH
AVGEETATZ
CARASSTAN
NAGDEECHESH
BATRATZTAG

CHAKVETNAH
YAGLEFZOK
SHAKUTZIT
NATZAREE-ELL
OZEE-ELL

It won't take you long to learn these eleven names, and then you are ready to activate the banishing. You don't even need to learn them by heart – just be able to say them, with clear confidence.

Before you can perform the banishing itself, there is a short activation that takes just a few moments, and this gives the banishing power for all future use. This activation needs to be performed just once, ever.

It is easy to do and is in fact so easy that you may think it's unimportant. Please do not skip this section. Although it only takes a few seconds, this small preparation makes the angels aware of your call so they can assist you in every banishing you perform for the rest of your life.

Find a time when you can be alone and a place where you can speak the words out loud. If you have to whisper them, imagine that you are calling them to the ends of the Universe.

At the end of this chapter, there is a sigil, in the form of a box, with the eleven names you have learned to speak. They are written in Hebrew and below that in English. To activate this magick simply look at each Hebrew word, in turn, scanning the letters from *right to left*. (This is the opposite direction to the way you read English.) You are not trying to read the words; you are just taking in the letter shapes as you scan over them. After you scan each word from *right to left*, you say the word beneath it. This word is read as a normal English word, from *left to right*, and you speak it out loud, three times.

Move down the list and scan the next word visually, and then read out the English word below it, three times. Continue until you have visually scanned and spoken all the words. They are now activated and ready for use in the banishing.

To ensure you understand this clearly, I will describe it once more, step by step:

Scan your eyes over the following sigil, looking at the uppermost Hebrew word, scanning your eyes from *right to left*. You are not trying to read or understand. You are only looking at the letter shapes.

Then repeat YOHACH at least three times. You can keep repeating it for up to a minute if you feel an urge to do so.

When that is done, move down one line and scan the second Hebrew word, from *right to left*, and then repeat KALACH at least three times, but for up to a minute if you want to.

You now have the attention of the angels and need to seal their commitment to you by reading the remaining names.

Move to the third line, and scan the third Hebrew word, from right to left, and repeat AVGEETATZ at least three times, but for up to a minute if you want to.

Continue in the same way, one line at a time, until you finish with OZEE-ELL which is also read at least three times.

All four angels - Yohach, Kalach, Natzariel, and Oziel - are now committed to your protection.

Your voice is connected to the angelic names through divine power. There is no need to close this ritual. Just relax and know that the magick has worked.

יוהך

YOHACH

כלך

KALACH

אבגיתצ

AVGEETATZ

קרעשטנ

CARASSTAN

נגדיכש

NAGDEECHESH

בתרצתג

BATRATZTAG

חקבטנע

CHAKVETNAH

יגלפזק

YAGLEFZOK

שקוצית

SHAKUTZIT

נצריאל

NATZAREE-ELL

עוזיאל

OZEE-ELL

The hard work is done, and *The Sword Banishing* can now be carried out with ease.

As mentioned previously, you can perform this out loud or silently in public. So long as you can say the words, or imagine them clearly while following the other instructions, this will work.

You will be required to visualize some images, but it doesn't matter if you are hopeless at visualization. Simply picture things as best you can, and that is good enough. Visualization is not about making perfect mental pictures, so much as a sense of knowing. If I tell you to imagine the sun, you know what the sun looks like, or you have an idea about what the sun is. That's good enough.

Worrying about magick ruins magick, so don't worry about whether or not you can visualize well enough. Do the best you can, and it will work.

You can sit, kneel, stand or lie down, but don't do this while walking, driving or doing anything that requires your attention.

To begin, take a breath and imagine the sun, and feel its mighty power. Imagine the sun shrinking down, and as it shrinks, it moves toward your chest. It settles in your heart as a tiny, brilliant star.

Say (or think) the name of the angel YOHACH, and imagine a mighty angel standing on your right, facing the same direction that you are facing. Whatever image comes to mind for you is the right image, so long as the angel is standing on your right and facing in the same direction that you are. (If you are lying down, it will be facing in the direction of your feet.) The angel can appear like a traditional winged being, or a huge muscled warrior. Let any image you like arise, and it is fine if the image is different every time you do the banishing. Ensure that Yohach holds a huge, brilliant sword in each hand. One sword is held across Yohach's body for protection, and the other is pointed forward, ready to attack.

Now say (or think) the name of the angel KALACH and imagine a mighty angel standing on your left. Again, let any image you like arise, but ensure that Kalach holds a huge, brilliant sword in each hand. One sword is held across Kalach's body for protection, and the other is pointed forward, ready to attack.

The swords can appear in any style that you like, but the blade should be made of a metal so brilliant that it glows like starlight.

Say (or think) the angelic name NATZAREE-ELL and remember the star of light in your chest. As you say (or think) the word OZ-EE-ELL, the star expands to surround you. (You do not need to imagine these particular angels.)

As the star expands, it's like being inside a huge sphere of brilliant white, with your heart at the very center. The sphere should be large enough that you are entirely enclosed within it. It will pass through the floor, your chair if you are seated, or your bed if you are lying down. It will pass through other people if they are nearby. This is all fine. You can make the sphere as large as a house, or as large as a mountain if you like, but most people find it easier to imagine a sphere that's about twice the size that they are.

Imagine this sphere of starlight for only a moment, and then let it fade, as the angels on either side fade from view. The banishing is done.

This may sound complex, but with practice, the whole process can take as little as ten seconds. You can use this banishing at a moment's notice when you feel any need. You can also use it once each morning and once each night. Best results come from regular use, but don't let it feel like an obligation. It should feel wondrous.

The Master Protection Ritual

The Master Protection Ritual should be carried out for thirty-three consecutive days. If you cannot perform it every day, continue when you can until thirty-three days have been completed.

This ritual strengthens your sense of self and your divine right to protection. It deflects curses and attacks. This working also acts as an uncrossing ritual. If you have been cursed, hexed, attacked psychically (intentionally or by accident), or suffer from any type of crossed conditions, this ritual will make you safe.

The ritual is a good way to protect yourself generally in the real world. It ensures that you are less likely to be a victim of violence, random accidents, and bad luck.

The daily *Sword Banishing* will hold off attacks, but this *Master Protection Ritual* is a way of declaring to the Universe that you are expressing your will in the world and that you want to follow your path without harm coming to you or your loved ones. The ritual will ensure that you are strengthened with magick, that any crossed conditions are removed, and that you have the power to carry out other Protection Rituals.

For many, this *Master Protection Ritual* is all you will need, and the remaining rituals will not be required. In some cases, though, highly potent attacks or difficult circumstances will require you to use the other Protection Rituals in the book. For now, know that this *Master Protection Ritual* is an extremely powerful way to assert your divine right to security and happiness and that it will give you protection, strength, and safety.

You will need the following talisman:

It can be used in the book, photocopied from the book, used directly on an iPad or any other e-book reader, or even a computer screen. If you want, you can download it and print it out from the images page on The Gallery of Magick website.

Before you begin, perform *The Sword Banishing*, even if you have already performed it today.

Place the talisman before you and take a few moments to think about the state you are in and how you currently feel. Be honest about your feelings, but observe them dispassionately. If you feel tense about an argument you've just had, notice that tension, but don't judge it or wish it away. Simply notice the feeling that is most prominent for you. If you feel bad, that's fine. If you feel great, that's fine as well. You simply need to take a moment to sense your actual emotional state.

Now scan your eyes over the letter shapes in the outer ring of the talisman, from *right to left*, starting at the very top and going anti-clockwise. This means you'll be scanning your eyes over letters that are upside down when you get to the bottom of the circle, and that is absolutely fine. You are not reading, but letting the letters sink into your eyes, effortlessly. These are words of power based on divine names. Keep moving your eyes over them, anti-clockwise, until you've seen each word.

Look at the top of the black star. Look at each letter in the black star, again starting at the top and moving anti-clockwise. These letters spell the names of the angels Yohach and Kalach, and this helps them to oversee the working.

Now gaze at the central triangle, without trying to read or scan the letters – just gaze at the white triangle. If you see the letters or feel drawn to look at them, that is fine, but just gaze at the white triangle for a few moments.

You have opened a gateway to a group of spirits that will hear your call. When you speak the following ritual, say it as though you mean it, and say it as though you are actually talking *to* somebody. Don't just read the words, but when you call on Haven, know that you are talking to a genius spirit known as Haven, who can grant you the powers of magick. Speak with authority. You are politely commanding, rather than begging or praying. The spirits have free will but will obey you gladly because the talisman has given you the divine authority to command them.

After speaking each line, pause for a moment, and think about what it would be like to have the power granted to you now, this very moment.

When you ask for 'the power of the magus,' imagine that you have been granted that power; the power to do magick.

When you ask for 'the power of harmony,' imagine the feeling of having that power; to bring harmony into your life.

This may take some practice, and the feelings you generate in these moments will change with time, but *always, always* pause after speaking the line, to feel as though the request has already been granted, and imagine what it feels like to have that power now.

This is the ritual. Say:

> Haven (HAH-VEN), genius of dignity,
> grant me the power of the magus.

> Baglis (BAH-GLISS), genius of measure and balance,
> grant me the power to express my will.

> Hahabi (HAH-HABI), genius of fear,
> let the force of my will overcome all terrors.

> Phalgus (FAL-GUSS), genius of judgment,
> grant me clear sight on the path to victory.

> Camaysar (CAH-MAY-SAR),
> genius of the marriage of contraries,
> grant me harmony.

> Tabris (TAH-BRIS), genius of free will,
> grant me power over my own domain.

> Sabrus (SAH-BRUS), sustaining genius,
> grant me the power to see beauty.

> Alphun (AL-FUN), genius of the doves,
> grant me peace.

> Zeffak (ZEFF-AK), genius of irrevocable choice,
> grant me the power to create my own immortality.

> Mastho (MAST-OH), genius of delusive appearances,
> grant me the power to see through all deception.

> Eglun (EGG-LUN), genius of lightning,

grant me the power to express my will through magick.

Marnes (MARN-EZ), genius of the discernment of spirits, grant me the power to protect myself.

Breathe for a moment or two, know that you are protected, and then close the book or put the talisman aside. The ritual is complete.

These genius spirits are often described as *personified virtues* and are known as *The Genii of the Twelve Hours*. They were described in the *Nuctemeron*, attributed to Apollonius of Tyana from the First Century AD. There is some confusion regarding these spirits, with some people assuming that 'genius' is the same as 'genie' because it sounds similar. Genies are also known as 'djinn' or 'jinn,' and they are sometimes unpredictable and evil. As such, I would never use them in this book. The misunderstanding occurs partly because of issues with translation, and because 'genius' sounds somewhat like 'genie.' With sufficient research, it is clear that the spirits employed in this ritual are gentle and safe.

It is my belief that these genius spirits are not angels, but are an embodiment of angelic power. That is, they personify the virtues of various angels in the form of unique spirits.

People who have actually used this magick report real and lasting results, so don't let armchair occultists who wrongly assume that 'genius' means 'genie' put you off. The genius spirits give you access to power that is as warm, safe and mighty as that of the angels because it is inspired and powered *by* angels.

Do not over-think this ritual. You only need to look at the talisman, say the words and imagine that you have been granted those qualities. Protection begins immediately and strengthens over the thirty-three days.

The Protection Rituals

The remainder of this book is split into two sections, each containing a variety of directed protection rituals.

Angelic Protection gives you a simple method to protect yourself from unwanted situations, using nothing more than a simple talisman and words of power. It is similar to the technique used in my popular *Words of Power* book.

Workings of Protection contains rituals for highly specific purposes. Some of these are short and simple, others more complex.

You may want to use several protections at once. If you feel the need, then you can begin several rituals on the same day, but you may find it easier to focus and concentrate if you work on one ritual at a time. Trust your intuition.

Angelic Protections

The following seven rituals each contain a talisman like this one:

There is a ring of words around the outside, written in Hebrew. These words appear almost identical, but each one calls on a different angel. In the center of the star are two words. One is a word of power to activate the ritual. The second one is the name of the angel.

Below the image, you will see a list of Words of Power. If you've used the *Words of Power* book, this is very similar, but please read these instructions, as there are some slight variations.

When you've chosen the ritual that you want to use, perform *The Sword Banishing* and sit alone in a quiet place. Spend some time thinking about the problem you want to stop, or the protection you need. You may find negative feelings get stirred up as you think about the problem. That's completely fine.

After a few moments, scan your eyes over the circle of letters on the outside of the talisman, starting at the top and moving from *right to left,* anticlockwise. You're not reading but *scanning* the letters. You're letting them sink into your consciousness, and that is enough.

You don't need to turn the talisman around to scan the words. It's fine to look at the words upside down when you get to the bottom of the image. When you have scanned all the words around the edge of the circle, pause for a moment, and then imagine what it would feel like if you had the protection you wanted.

In some cases, this will be a feeling of relief or clarity. If, for example, you are using the ritual to Cleanse a Space, you might imagine how good it will feel to rid the room or house of those negative energies.

Sometimes, the feeling will be more like security. If you're doing magick to protect your job, then you can imagine what it would feel like to know that your job is absolutely secure. It would be a good feeling, so let it rise up.

Once you have that sense of the result already being achieved, look at the words in the center of the talisman. You do not need to read them or scan them, but simply gaze at them, and let the shapes of the letters be absorbed into your mind. As you do this, let your feelings turn to gratitude, as though the magick has already worked. This feeling of gratitude can arise directly from the feelings of relief, security, and protection you just created.

Don't try to imagine how the protection will work, or what circumstances need to change. Simply concentrate on the feeling of gratitude you have now that the protection is in place. Know that the words you are about to speak will thank the angel that performs the work for you.

Speak the words of power. These are written below each talisman, and they are read as standard English, from left to right. They are almost the same for each ritual. The words that are different are written in bold.

The very first word is a divine name that activates the magick. The second word is the angel that is called upon in the ritual. You will see that the angel name appears again as you keep reading the words. Before you say the words, know that you are calling on this angel to bring protection and that you are offering gratitude in advance.

While reading the words out loud simply feel grateful that the protection you desire is already in place.

If you are alone and can say the words loudly, let them vibrate through your throat. It's as though you are breathing the words out, letting them rumble up from your belly through the back of your throat. It's almost like chanting or singing them.

This 'vibration' where you let the words rumble out of you is not essential and will be impossible for many, so if need be, just say them out loud. If you can't say them out loud, whisper them or imagine them, but imagine they are being bellowed out to the ends of the Universe.

Sometimes you may sense a response from the angel, but often you will feel nothing. It doesn't matter, so long as you hold on to the feeling of gratitude as you say the words.

When you have said the final word, you can close the book and go about your business. Try not to think about the results or how they will come about. Look at the articles on my website for details on 'lust for result' to ensure that you don't short-circuit the magick, and you'll get the protection you need.

Please read the details for each ritual, to see how many days it needs to be performed for. When you've carried out the ritual for the set number of days, stop, to show your faith in the magick.

I've described the process in detail to make sure you have all the knowledge you need, but here is a brief summary:

1. Choose the ritual you want and then perform *The Sword Banishing*.

2. Think about the problem you face and the protection you need. Allow your feelings about this to arise. The feelings may be fearful or angry, or they may be more like wishes and desires for protection.

3. While holding onto these feelings scan your eyes around the ring of words on the talisman, starting at the top, scanning anti-clockwise.

4. Pause and imagine how it would feel if the magick worked. How would it feel if you had the protection you seek?

5. When you can imagine how good it would be to have the result, gaze at the words in the center of the talisman. As you do this, let your feelings turn into gratitude. Be grateful that the angel is offering you the protection you seek.

6. Speak the words of power below the talisman, reading them like English, from left to right. Feel grateful that the protection you desire is already in place.

7. Close the book and do something that stops you thinking about magick for a while. Do not wonder how the magick will work or when it will work.

8. Repeat for the set number of days. If you miss a day, simply continue when you can until you've performed the ritual for the specified number of days.

The protection you seek will now be in place. Continue with a daily *Sword Banishing*.

Remove Parasitic Beings

There are many types of parasitic entities that can attach to you, from supernatural beings to energy-sapping people. A parasite is something that feeds off your energy. If you feel the presence of an entity that is haunting you, or if there is a person in your life that drains you of energy, this ritual will stop them.

Supernatural parasites come in many forms, but unless you're very unlucky, you will only encounter one if you are involved in advanced magick. If that applies to you, use this ritual. This ritual, however, is really aimed at stopping the ordinary people who drain energy from you. Sometimes, people drain your energy deliberately, and other times they have no idea they are doing it. These people are sometimes thought of as energy vampires, and if you have one in your life, you will know about it.

A parasitic person will be needy, demanding and will make you feel less like yourself, with less control over your desires and decisions. You may feel weak and foggy-headed around them, giving in to their demands and requests. You may not notice the effect while the person is around, but when they have gone, you may sense that you have been drained.

If you suspect that somebody drains your energy, deliberately or otherwise, use this ritual. This will not remove the person from your life or harm them; it will stop them feeding off your energy. If you use it on a person who's doing nothing wrong, don't worry, it won't harm that person at all.

When scanning the ring of words, picture the person and think of their name, but do not say it out loud. Apart from that, carry out the ritual exactly as described earlier. If you are performing this to get rid of a supernatural being, simply be aware of the feeling it creates in you, and hold onto that feeling as you scan the ring of words. Perform the ritual for five days.

CRASTAN
SHAM-SHE-ELL
YEAH-HEE RATS-ON MILL-FAN-ECHA
EH-YEAH ASHER EH-YEAH
UMILL-FAN-ECHA HA-MAL-ACH
SHAM-SHE-ELL
VEB-SHEM YAG-ALP-ZAK
SHER-TATS-LEE-ACH
BUR-CAM-EE-AH ZEH

Cleanse any Space

Sometimes a place just doesn't feel right. It might be that it's haunted, that you've attracted some unwanted supernatural attention, or that the energy there is just not good. There are thousands of reasons why this can happen, but sometimes a room, house or even a whole area of land can feel disturbing.

If you find yourself feeling uneasy or afraid in any space that you go to regularly, this ritual will provide relief from that feeling. You need to be in that space when you perform the ritual.

Perform the ritual for three days.

BAG-EE-TATZ
YO-FEE-ELL
YEAH-HEE RATS-ON MILL-FAN-ECHA
EH-YEAH ASHER EH-YEAH
UMILL-FAN-ECHA HA-MAL-ACH
YO-FEE-ELL
VEB-SHEM YAG-ALP-ZAK
SHER-TATS-LEE-ACH
BUR-CAM-EE-AH ZEH

Protect Your Job

Many people are afraid of losing their jobs, and this ritual will ensure you don't lose yours. It's best to use this only if you are fearful of losing your job and believe that job losses might be around the corner.

Why not just use it to be on the safe side? Because this ritual ensures that you will keep your job, that can mean you stay in the same job – which rules out a promotion or other interesting career developments.

This ritual is priceless if you are certain you want to keep your job for now, but use it with caution if you are looking to develop your career.

To avoid career stagnation, the effect of the ritual only lasts for approximately three months. If you want to protect your job for a full year, you will need to perform it four times a year.

If you are self-employed and want to hold onto a particular contractor or customer, you can use this ritual to get the desired result. Think about that contractor or customer as you scan the circle of words.

You only need to perform this ritual for two days.

BUH-TAR TZA-TAG
RACH-ME-ELL
YEAH-HEE RATS-ON MILL-FAN-ECHA
EH-YEAH ASHER EH-YEAH
UMILL-FAN-ECHA HA-MAL-ACH
RACH-ME-ELL
VEB-SHEM YAG-ALP-ZAK
SHER-TATS-LEE-ACH
BUR-CAM-EE-AH ZEH

Protect Your Business

At one stage we developed rituals to protect all aspects of a business, from making sure the tax filing was legal to ensuring that the business remained competitive. After some time, we simplified this into the ritual you find here. This single ritual will protect your business from bankruptcy, theft, bad employees, bad debtors, legal problems and cash flow difficulties.

Although the ritual is exceptionally powerful, you must remember that you need to do your share of the work. If you act irresponsibly, waste money, promote your work badly or do a shoddy job, your business cannot be saved by magick. If, however, you are like most businesses – working hard and aiming to thrive – this ritual will give you protection from unwanted trouble and financial difficulties.

When picturing the protection that you want, you can think quite generally about keeping your business safe, secure and thriving. If you have a particularly pressing or specific business problem such as a bad debtor or a legal issue, you can think about that specifically.

Carry out this ritual for nine days.

SHUH-KAV TZUH-YAT
CARVE-EE-ELL
YEAH-HEE RATS-ON MILL-FAN-ECHA
EH-YEAH ASHER EH-YEAH
UMILL-FAN-ECHA HA-MAL-ACH
CARVE-EE-ELL
VEB-SHEM YAG-ALP-ZAK
SHER-TATS-LEE-ACH
BUR-CAM-EE-AH ZEH

Protect Against Accidents

Accidents happen, and no ritual can prevent them all from happening. This ritual, though, is one I really like because it's got me out of a lot of near-misses. When accidents have happened, they haven't been so bad. And I've avoided a lot of situations that *should* have been accidents. It felt like I was saved by an angel at the last moment, and that's because I *was*.

If you are afraid of accidents, or if you live in a city with particularly bad drivers, or work in a profession that's dangerous, or have hobbies that involve risks, this is a great ritual to use. Even if you live a fairly ordinary life, you might want to protect yourself anyway.

You can think about being generally protected from accidents, or you can direct this to give you extra protection in a dangerous profession or sport while scanning the ring of words.

The magick can be shared easily. If you want to protect your loved ones, you can simply think about protecting them as you read the ring of words, and feel relief and gratitude that they are protected.

The ritual should be carried out for eleven days, and then repeated every year. It's also worth repeating if you take up a hobby or job that introduces new dangers into your life.

BAG-EE-TATZ
OAR-PA-KNEE-ELL
YEAH-HEE RATS-ON MILL-FAN-ECHA
EH-YEAH ASHER EH-YEAH
UMILL-FAN-ECHA HA-MAL-ACH
OAR-PA-KNEE-ELL
VEB-SHEM YAG-ALP-ZAK
SHER-TATS-LEE-ACH
BUR-CAM-EE-AH ZEH

Protection from Stalkers

This might sound like an obscure ritual, but many people suffer from stalking, especially now that the internet gives stalkers easier ways to keep track of you and your movements.

If you are actually being stalked and harassed by a person, go to the police.

This ritual should be used when you sense that somebody is starting to give you more attention than you want, and when their behavior begins to feel out of place or mildly disturbing. It's one way to stop that person turning into a stalker. If you already have a stalker harassing you, in the real world or online, use the ritual immediately.

It helps if you know the name and face of the person who is stalking you. If you do, picture the face and think of the name as you scan the ring of words. If you do not know who's stalking you – say, if you're getting offensive emails or Facebook messages – simply think about the feeling that person creates when you are harassed by them.

The ritual does no harm to the person, so feel free to use it on mildly creepy individuals who are paying you too much attention, as well as more threatening types who verge on the dangerous.

Carry out the ritual for five days.

NUH-GAD EE-CHASH
KAV-SHE-ELL
YEAH-HEE RATS-ON MILL-FAN-ECHA
EH-YEAH ASHER EH-YEAH
UMILL-FAN-ECHA HA-MAL-ACH
KAV-SHE-ELL
VEB-SHEM YAG-ALP-ZAK
SHER-TATS-LEE-ACH
BUR-CAM-EE-AH ZEH

Protection Against Unwanted Attention

Many people report that it is impossible to go out at night – to parties, bars, and nightclubs - without getting creepy, offensive and intrusive attention from others. This sort of unwanted attention ranges from creepy looks to rude comments and even subtle physical assaults.

This ritual has been developed to protect people of both sexes, to deflect behavior that is rude, frightening or simply unappealing. It helps you to ward off unwanted and dangerous attention but also increases your awareness of people who might cause trouble. You can then steer clear of them. It won't make you paranoid, but will just give you a clear instinct about unsavory people.

I would never want you to let your guard down because of magick. If you go to a wild party and leave your drink for even a moment, it can still be spiked. Use this ritual with caution and remain as alert as ever.

Those who have used it say that it has made for more pleasant evenings. Thankfully, it does not work by making you invisible to all onlookers. It makes you less interesting to people who are aggressive or troublesome.

If you are going to a social occasion looking for a date, you can safely use this ritual – it won't hide you away. It will only repel the sort of person that would be pushy or annoying to you.

The ritual only needs to be performed once, and the effect will last for about a year. You can then repeat it if required.

If you want to protect a specific group of friends on a specific occasion, you can perform the ritual on that day, and imagine protection for yourself and all your friends. You do not need to tell them about it, and as with most magick, it's probably best if you don't.

EE-GAL-PUH-ZAK
LA-HA-VEE-ELL
YEAH-HEE RATS-ON MILL-FAN-ECHA
EH-YEAH ASHER EH-YEAH
UMILL-FAN-ECHA HA-MAL-ACH
LA-HA-VEE-ELL
VEB-SHEM YAG-ALP-ZAK
SHER-TATS-LEE-ACH
BUR-CAM-EE-AH ZEH

The Workings of Protection

The following Workings of Protection all use exceptionally rare and powerful talismans.

At the start of each ritual, perform *The Sword Banishing*.

The process for each working is slightly different, but every ritual contains the process of Igniting the Talisman.

This part of the process is quite simple, and the talismans have been printed in black, with white letters to make the visualization process easier.

To ignite a talisman, you gaze at the whole shape of the talisman first. If it is a diamond, look at it as a black diamond. If it is a circle, see the black circle. Simply gaze passively at the black shape. You will notice lines and letters, but you do not need to pay attention to them.

After gazing at the talisman for about ten seconds, you should turn your attention to the white lines and letters. Look at all the lines and letters without staring, but look at them with more focus than before. It doesn't matter what order you do this in, only that you see every letter and shape that is before you. You are not trying to read or understand. This is a way of letting the talisman sink into your consciousness.

To ignite the talisman, gaze at it without focusing on the letters, but allow the letters to glow bright white. It is as though diamond starlight is passing through the letters and shapes. Let bright light shine through.

Even if you don't have a good imagination, you should get some sense of white starlight shining through the talisman. (If your imagination is terrible, it doesn't matter – just pretend that light is coming through. It works if you pretend with the same commitment that a child would use when pretending!)

For some rituals, you have the option to use printed talismans as part of the operation. When that is the case, you can find the required talismans at The Gallery of Magick website. If you have a printed copy of the book, you can photocopy the pages and use those as your talismans.

Note that when you read the following workings, the description may say, 'Now ignite the talisman and...' When you read such words, it means that you should carry out the procedure described in this chapter.

Stop a Known Enemy

Sometimes you know exactly who your enemy is, and you want to stop them. That doesn't mean you want to curse them or cause them harm, but you want to stop that person from harming you. This can apply to anybody from a boss you loathe to a rude neighbor or a colleague who undermines you. It can even apply to a family member. There are times when the people we love are cruel to us and become enemies for a time. Enemies can apply subtle harm or wreck your life. Whatever the case, you can stop their attacks without causing them any harm.

The ritual can be used against anybody that you believe is harming you, and it will stop them. It does this by taking away their will to harm you and makes them lose interest in causing you pain. It can even be used within a relationship to make a partner who has become thoughtless, act with more care.

Find a quiet place where you will have a few minutes to yourself. Know that the angel Yohach is named in this talisman, and Yohach will help to empower the working.

Spend a few moments thinking about the person you consider to be your enemy. Think of the things they have done. Do not try to determine whether their actions were fair or justified. Only think about how you felt, and your reaction to these incidents. Whether this person makes casual rude remarks or tries to ruin your life, think through the problems until you have a strong feeling about the harm this person has caused you. Think about how much you want to put a stop to your pain.

Look at the talisman.

Now imagine how good it would feel if your enemy stopped hurting you this very moment. Ignite the talisman, as described earlier. While igniting the talisman, feel grateful that the protection is in place and that your enemy is disarmed. Allow that relief to feel real for a few moments, and then you can close the book and continue with your day.

You need to repeat this for three days, but on each day there is a slight variation.

On the first day, when you let your feelings and thoughts build, really think about all the ways that the person has hurt you, and even allow yourself to feel anger, shame, disgust, hatred or any other strong negative emotions.

On the second day, ease some of the emotion out of this. List the things that the person has done to you in your mind, and let your emotions arise as they will, but don't let yourself get too worked up; keep the emotions under control. Feel gratitude that their power to harm you has been taken away as you ignite the talisman.

On the third day, think about this person's actions against you, but consider their actions as nothing more than a foolish mistake. Your enemy should not have tried to attack you. Know this and then feel gratitude that they have been stopped as you ignite the talisman.

The magick is complete unless you are dealing with a particularly offensive and cruel enemy. There are times when people dislike you a great deal and deliberately use every opportunity to hurt you. This can happen within families, at work, and in other social situations. If you feel that somebody has effectively declared war on you, even if nobody else can see the harm that's being done, you can add a second working to ensure that your enemy is rendered utterly harmless.

The second working is quite involved and requires you to get access to the enemy's property (legally), so this magick is not for everybody. The first working will be enough unless there is real hatred or enmity, so only use this second part of the ritual if you really need to.

If you do choose to go ahead with this, know that this is powerful angelic magick that aims to end a war between two people. Even though the methods may seem unusual and extreme, this is one of the most powerful ways to bring peace between enemies.

When you have completed the first three days of the working, you can wait a while to see how the magick has worked, or you can begin this second working the next day.

Print out four copies of this talisman.

Ignite each copy of the talisman, one at a time, while picturing your enemy, and allow feelings about your enemy to arise.

Now take each talisman and roll each it into a tiny ball of paper. You need to get these four individual pieces of paper onto the property where your enemy lives, in a way that they will not be discovered. If you live in the property, with the person, it couldn't be much easier, but real enemies usually live somewhere else.

I should say that you must do this working within the confines of the law, or you are giving your enemy an opportunity to shame you, or even have you arrested. You do not want to break laws, and you do not want to get caught.

You should discreetly enclose the balls of paper in small pieces of clay. I use a product called Daz Pronto, available at modeling shops, because it dries in the air, quickly. You can use a similar product, or you can use anything that acts like clay. I know one magickal worker who used marzipan, but I don't recommend that, as you don't want anybody to eat your magickal workings by mistake.

If you cannot find a good substitute for clay, the other option is to wet the paper and mash it up, then let it dry into a small hard ball.

Whether you use clay, water or something else, you will be left with four tiny balls that need to make their way onto your enemy's home property. Make sure they are dry before you begin.

It's not too difficult to throw them into an enemy's garden, but be aware that many people have CCTV installed, and that deliberately littering their property is possibly illegal.

Here are the options I prefer to use:

Option 1: Visit the enemy. Often, our real enemies are people we are entwined with, and so a visit is nothing out of the ordinary. My former mother-in-law was a truly cruel woman, but I had easy access to her house. While visiting, it was easy to dispose of the four clay 'stones' around the house, pushing them into the pot-plant soil, putting them onto the top of cupboards where they were out of sight, and so on.

Option 2: Post something to the enemy – such as a lovely book or gift – anonymously, and package it with scrunched up newspaper. Hide your 'stones' inside the newspaper. They will almost certainly stay on the property for 24 hours. If you know what day the trash is collected from that property, it's even easier to make sure the talisman stones will remain in place for a full day.

Option 3: Jog past (in a subtle disguise) and hurl the clay stones over the fence, into the garden. Risky and possibly illegal, but still the one I like best. I don't really advise this one, even though I've done it reasonably often. (If you ever do anything like this, use the sort of misdirection that a card magician would use. Magicians always hide a small secret move with a larger move, so that the eye is directed to the unimportant movement. If your right hand is flicking the stones over the fence, simultaneously bring up your left hand to run it through your hair. Even if somebody's watching you closely, they will follow the large motion of your innocent left hand, not the small motion of your right hand as it flicks the stones away.)

If none of these methods are going to work, you can think of your own, or there is a final method I can suggest. Instead of making the clay stones, carefully burn the talismans, taking extreme care not to burn yourself or set fire to your house. When the ashes have cooled, mix them into a small amount of water. Stir well, and you should have a few drops of black water. Pour this outside the door of your enemy, so that when they leave the house, they will tread in the ashes. Pure ash blows away, but the liquid form tends to stick.

This working is far more involved than most of the magick I use, so only use this second half of the ritual if there is an absolute war between you and the other party. In most cases, the first part of the ritual is all you will need.

Cancel a Curse or Supernatural Attack

If you fear that you have been cursed or are experiencing a supernatural attack, this is the most powerful method I know to repel a curse, when used in conjunction with *The Sword Banishing* and *The Master Protection Ritual*.

The only catch is that you have to work with this talisman for thirty-three days. Curses can be casual and yet powerful. They can be carefully constructed and filled with defenses. Supernatural attacks take many forms, and can even come from nothing more than sheer hatred. As such, you need to repel the curse for thirty-three days. If you suspect that you have been cursed, or if you feel that somebody wishes you great harm or sense that any spell or magickal work has been set against you, use the talisman for thirty-three days.

At any time during the day or night, find a time when you can be alone and undisturbed. Quiet helps. Do not think about the details of the curse – the events that have happened, or the evidence you have of supernatural attack – but think about what it *feels like* to be cursed. Notice any physical or emotional sensations this brings up. Now ignite the talisman as described earlier. This is quite a detailed talisman, so take the time to let the light shine through every white part of the image. As you do so, the feeling of the curse should lift slightly.

After you've been working with this for a week, you should begin to treat the curse as a memory rather than something that is ongoing, so think about how it *used to feel* to be cursed, then ignite the talisman and let the feeling of relief come. Act as though the curse is something in your past even if you see evidence of the curse being present in your life. Pushing it into the past in this way, with a deliberate act of imagination, is extremely powerful and untangles the complexities that can hold a curse in place.

In most cases, this is all you will need, and the curse will be gone.

If you still see evidence of a curse when thirty-three days are up, it may be that you are being repeatedly attacked. This is very rare, but as mentioned before, it has happened to me. It happens so rarely that I hardly even want to mention it, but if you see obvious evidence of a repeated attack, simply begin again. Repeat for thirty-three days, and eventually, your attacker will give up. When used a second time on the same person or group, the talisman works even faster and can render future attempts at cursing you futile. It doesn't just stop the attack but prevents new attacks from occurring.

If you are ever cursed, it's highly unlikely you'll need to use this more than once.

Become Less Conspicuous

There are many times when you may want to be less conspicuous. Although this type of magick is used by criminals to avoid being observed by the authorities, I don't recommend that you use it for that type of work. Keep it legal. The real purpose of this magick is to make you less noticeable when you feel you are being observed too closely by somebody who could bring you harm.

In particular, this magick is useful in messy divorce cases, or when any relationship ends. It can make the other person lose interest in you rapidly, rather than have them monitoring your every move.

You will become less conspicuous to all people, but if you aim the ritual at a specific person, most of the energy will be directed there. You can even aim it at the particular department of a company. Imagine that Human Resources have their eye on you and want to fire some workers. You have a choice. You can make yourself shine radiantly and try to show how worthy you are of keeping the job, or if you would rather be off their radar, use this talisman against the whole Human Resources department, and they'll barely notice that you exist.

This magick will have the effect of making you generally less noticeable in the world. Friends may pass you in the street, for example. If your job involves being famous or visible in some way, this magick should be used only when needed.

Thankfully, you can tune the magick to work for the exact length of time that you need it to work. If you only want it to work for a day, it will work for a day. If you need a month or a year, you can get that.

All you need to do is think about a period of time as you ignite the talisman (as described earlier). Think about the coming day, week, month, year or whatever length of protection you want. You don't even need to think about the actual protection you're seeking. Just think about a period of time and ignite the talisman. That will do the work.

If you want more than a year, you should repeat the magick in twelve months.

If there's a particular person, department or organization that you want to remain hidden from, you should also picture that person, department or organization clearly, and think about their name while igniting the talisman. Again, you do not need to think about being less conspicuous – just think about the target of your magick and the length of time you want it to work for.

Protection Against Hacking and Identity Theft

This is a talisman that we developed ourselves, based on an ancient amulet, to call on entities that are directly connected to electricity and communication. We have found that it works extremely well at protecting you from any form of hacking or identity theft.

The talisman was created because, despite using all the protection magick that we already use, many of us experienced various forms of credit card fraud and identity theft in the past decade. Since we started using this talisman, two years ago, nobody has been affected. As with all our work, it has been field-tested by a trusted group of occultists, and all have had the same results.

As always, you should make sure you do everything you can in the mundane world to secure your computer and protect your identity.

To activate the talisman, you should think about all the computer devices you use, from iPads to laptops, public computers, and WiFi connections. Think about the sort of places you use credit cards or services such as PayPal. Consider this for just a minute or so, dispassionately – you do not need to create any emotion. Now ignite the talisman, using the process described earlier, and as you do so, know that your identity is protected wherever you interact with electronic devices.

We aren't certain how long this protection lasts, so we suggest repeating it once a year.

כל הנשמה תהלל

כהת
חשמל

חיות אש ממללול

של בחשך

Protection While Traveling

When you travel, you need protection from theft, accidents, illness, delays, getting lost, losing documents and many other kinds of inconvenience. I travel a lot, so I use this talisman every time I set out on a journey that's going to last more than a day.

It is one of the simplest talismans to activate. Two days before your journey begins, picture the journey you are going to embark upon. Ignite the talisman and continue to picture the journey. You do not need to perform a visualization covering every detail. Simply imagine arriving at your destination, traveling from place to place, and returning home in one piece with a smile on your face. This should take less than three minutes. Even if you don't know exactly where you're going, as is often the case, just picture a rough approximation of your journey. It will still work.

Perform the ritual for two days before you leave, and then for a third time just moments before you leave your house. If that's not possible, find a time during the early part of your journey to activate the talisman for the third time.

If you go on a last-minute trip and have no time to prepare, activate the talisman as described, on each of the first three days.

Some people also activate the talisman once more, the day before the return flight or the start of the return journey. I have never felt the need to do so, but the option is there if it makes you feel better. Again, just picture the remainder of your journey with the required images as you ignite the talisman.

Protection from Violence

This ritual is aimed at protecting you from violence, especially if you live in a rough area, or have to pass through one. It can also be used to reduce the chance of violence in the home, but when it comes to domestic violence, I always suggest getting out of there and getting to the police before you do anything else.

I do know some people, however, who have told me that it takes time to plan an escape from a violent relationship, and so a talisman like this can be used during that time, so long as your aim is to get away from the source of violence. The main aim of the talisman is to prevent people from attacking you physically or verbally. It can protect you from robbery, road rage and assaults of all kinds.

To activate the talisman, spend some time in a quiet place thinking about the dangers you have seen, or the things you fear, or the particular person you are afraid of. Let your emotions rise up, even if they are strongly negative. Experience the fear and know that you want it to be gone.

Now imagine how good it would feel if the talisman offered you a complete shield against violence. Ignite the talisman as described earlier and feel grateful for the safety it offers. Imagine going to the places you have feared, or being with the people you have feared, and as the talisman glows, feel grateful that you are now protected.

This should take about two minutes, and you should repeat this for eleven days.

As always, don't go looking for trouble or take risks, but if you simply go about your business, this talisman will keep you safe.

82

Some people live in genuinely war-torn areas and need extreme protection. The following talisman is meant to protect civilians who live in violent or war-torn places. It will not protect those who are fighting, so only use it if you are a civilian living in an area that is plagued by war, gangs or mobs of any description.

The process is the same as above. Picture the violence you fear, imagine how good it would be to have a shield of protection, ignite the talisman, and for two minutes feel grateful for the safety you are now experiencing. This ritual should be repeated for three days every month.

Stop Gossip and Rumors

This talisman can be used to stop gossip and rumors. Apart from being unpleasant, rumors can ruin your reputation and damage your career. Gossip can make you unattractive to people, and sadly, when people spread lies about you, other people will often believe those lies. Liars should be silenced.

There are two ways to use this talisman. If you know that a specific person is spreading false stories about you or generally slandering you, visualize that person talking. Picture them telling lies about you and let your anger and disgust build. Then imagine that person's mouth freezing up so they can no longer speak. This should make you feel some relief, so ignite the talisman, using the process described earlier, and feel grateful that the gossip has been stopped.

If you know that lies are being spread, but you don't know the source, or if you suspect several people are talking about you unfairly, repeat the above exercise, but instead of picturing a specific person, simply bring up your own feelings and the pain you experience when you know that lies are being told. Then imagine the relief of having the gossip cease. Ignite the talisman using the method described earlier, as you feel gratitude for the power of the magick.

Whichever method you use, repeat this for three days.

Take Power from a Bully

There are bullies at work, home and even within groups of friends. Bullies might be direct, loud, or so subtle that nobody would ever believe you if you spoke up about being victimized.

Bullies are cowards who feed off your suffering. This talisman doesn't silence the bully directly or remove them from your life, but it makes the bully feel extremely confused about you. It will confuse their feelings into a mix of fear and admiration. The confusion takes away the bully's power, as they no longer feel like they have the upper hand. This is a crafty form of magick that works to disarm a bully quickly.

Picture the person who has bullied you as though they are standing directly in front of you. Imagine looking into their eyes. Imagine that person's name being spoken as a tiny whisper. Now imagine your own name being shouted out so loudly that it confuses the bully. Imagine your name literally thundering down from the heavens.

Ignite the talisman, using the process described earlier, and after about a minute picture the bully again, but now imagine that person being confused, looking around in bewilderment and then slowly turning around and walking away from you. Feel relief and gratitude as the bully walks away from you in confusion.

Perform this ritual for two days.

Protect Your Home

This ritual is designed to protect your home from thieves, but also to give it the best possible protection during storms and other incidents that could cause damage. It works whether you rent a room, share an apartment or live in a large house.

Sit in a quiet place in your home. Think about when you moved into the home and all the years that you have lived there. If you were born there, you might have a lot of memories, but this also works if you've only been there for one full day and night. You simply need to think about the time you have spent in the home and remember times that you have eaten there, slept there and times when other people have been in the house. This doesn't need to be detailed and only needs to take a minute or two. You are simply getting a feeling for your home.

Ignite the talisman as described earlier, and after about two minutes, imagine the light from the talisman beaming out to all the boundaries of your home – the walls, the ceiling, the floor. You can even extend this light outside, to the actual boundary of your property. Know that your home is protected by angelic power, and feel grateful for your safety, as you let the light of the talisman fade away.

Perform this ritual for three days and repeat it every year.

Protect Your Possessions from Thieves

This ritual protects the possessions you carry with you, such as phones, purses, wallets, packages, watches or anything else of value. The magick works by repelling thieves, so they don't even come near you.

Find a place where you can be alone and imagine holding three gold coins in your left hand. Close your hand around these imaginary coins so that your hand is a fist. Now ignite the talisman, using the method described earlier, and feel grateful that all the valuable objects you touch will remain within your grasp. This ritual can be performed in less than a minute.

Perform the ritual for eleven days and repeat it every three years.

If you are ever particularly concerned about a new item that you have purchased, you can repeat the ritual, and as you ignite the talisman, picture the new object held firmly in your hands and feel grateful that it is now safe.

Protection Against Influence

There are some people who can have too much influence on your life. This might be a domineering parent, a controlling partner, a co-worker, or just a friend that has a strong influence over you. This ritual will ensure that you are able to make your own decisions, without being overly influenced by others.

The ritual also works if you are the sort of person that is susceptible to the thoughts and feelings of others. Some people find that they pick up another person's mood – almost like catching a disease. Others find that they are so empathetic toward people that it's difficult to hold onto their own sense of identity. This ritual will ensure that you can retain any psychic abilities you have and remain empathetic, without losing your own sense of self.

Sit alone for a few minutes, and then simply ignite the talisman, using the method described earlier. This is probably the easiest of all the rituals. Keep the talisman lit up for about a minute. Perform the ritual for eleven days.

In most cases, the ritual does not need to be repeated, but you can do so at any time if you feel the need for a stronger sense of self.

Pronunciation Guide

Find a common English word that contains the sound that's written in capitals, and you will have the pronunciation you need. So, EE is like **ee** in the English **been**.

For the sake of clarity, here is a list of every magickal word in the book, with full details on pronunciation. Do not feel the need to go through and check everything. Only use this section if you are genuinely uncertain or uneasy about your pronunciation.

Remember that the CH sound is always like the *ch* in Scottish *loch* or German *achtung*. If you struggle, replace every spoken CH with a K.

For more guidance, see the audio/video guide on the *Pronunciation and Spelling FAQ* at The Gallery of Magick website.

Words from The Sword Banishing

YOHACH

Yohach is pronounced YO-HACH.

YO sounds like *no*, but with a *y* instead of an *n*.

HACH sounds similar to *hack*, but with the CH sound discussed in the previous chapter. If you struggle with the CH sound, then simply say *hack*.

After some practice, you should run these sounds together, so that you have YOHACH. If you struggle with the CH sound, then you can use YOHAK.

KALACH

Kalach is pronounced KAL-ACH.

KAL sounds like *pal* but with a *k* instead of a *p*.

ACH sounds like *back* without the *b*, using the CH sound discussed previously. If you struggle with the CH sounds, then you can simply say *ack*.

After some practice, you should run these sounds together, so that you have KALACH. If you struggle with the CH sound, then you can use KALAK.

These names are also used in the banishing:

AV-GEE-TATZ
AV sounds like the second half of *have*. GEE sounds like *bee* but with a *g*. TATZ is read as *tat* with a *z* sound at the end.

CAR-ASS-TAN
Car is pronounced like the beginning of *cart*. ASS sounds like *pass* without the *p*. TAN is read exactly as it sounds.

NAG-DEE-CHESH
NAG sounds exactly as spelled - *nag*. DEE sounds just like the letter *d*. CHESH begins with the CH sound discussed earlier in the chapter on pronunciation. ESH sounds like *mesh* without the *m*. If you struggle with the CH sound, replace CHESH with KESH.

BAT-RATZ-TAG
Bat sounds like *bat*. RATZ sounds like the English *rats* but with the s extended into a *z* sound. In most cases, saying *rats* is fine. TAG sounds like *tag*.

CHAK-VET-NAH

The CH sound is the pronunciation discussed earlier, followed by AK, which is like *jack* without the *j*. If you struggle with the CH sound, change the first part of the word to KAK. VET sounds as it is written. NAH rhymes with **bar**, but is extended slightly to sound like the *Ahhhh* you say when you see a beautiful baby, but with *n* at the beginning.

YAG-LEF-ZOK

YAG sounds like *bag* but with a *y* instead of a *b*. LEF sounds like the word *left* but without the *t*. ZOK rhymes with *sock*, but you start it with a *z* rather than an *s*.

SHAK-UT-ZIT

SHAK is the same as *shack*. UT sounds like *but* without the **b**, and ZIT is just the word *zit*.

NAT-ZAR-EE-ELL

NAT is *bat* with an *n*. ZAR is *car* with a *z*. EE is *bee* without the **b**. ELL is *bell* without the **b**.

OZ-EE-ELL

OZ is *was* without the *w*. EE is *bee* without the **b**. ELL is *bell* without the **b**.

Words from the Master Protection Ritual

HAH-VEN

HAH is like the English *ha*, but with a slightly elongated *ahhh* at the end. VEN is the same as *hen* but with a *v*.

BAH-GLISS

BAH is like *bar*, but with a slightly softer *r*, like the sound a sheep is supposed to make in storybooks. GLISS is like *bliss* with a *g*.

HAH-HABI

HAH is like the English *ha*, but with a slightly elongated *ahhh* at the end. HABI is like *flabby*, but starting with an *h* and with more of an *ee* ending.

FAL-GUSS

FAL is *pal* with an *f*. GUSS is *puss* with a *g*.

CAH-MAY-SAR

CAH is like *car*, but with a slightly elongated *ahhh* at the end. MAY is just *may*. SAR is like *star* without the *t*.

TAH-BRIS

TAH is like *tar*, but with a slightly elongated *ahhh* at the end. BRIS is like *bliss* with an *r* instead of the *l*.

SAH-BRUS

SAH is like *star* without the *t*, but with a slightly elongated *ahhh* at the end. BRUS is like the first part of *Brussels*.

AL-FUN

AL is *pal* without the *p*. FUN is just *fun*.

ZEFF-AK

ZEF is like the name *Geoff* with a *z*. AK is like *jack* without the *j*.

MAST-OH

MAST is just *mast*, and OH is just *oh*.

EGG-LUN

Egg is *egg*, and LUN is like *fun* with an *l* instead of an *f*.

MARN-EZ

MARN is like *barn* but with an *m*, and EZ is like the *es* sound in *resolution*.

Words from the Angelic Protections

The main words used for each talisman are as follows:

YEAH-HEE RATS-ON MILL-FAN-ECHA

All these words are said just like the English equivalents, apart from ECHA, which contains the CH sound described in the pronunciation chapter, and rhymes with *decker*.

EH-YEAH ASHER EH-YEAH

EH is like *yeah* without the *y*. ASHER is like *basher* without the *b*.

UMILL-FAN-ECHA HA-MAL-ACH

UMILL is like *yum* without the *y*, and *ill*. FAN and ECHA have been covered. HA-MAL-ACH sounds like English *ha*, then *pal* with an *m* instead of a *p*, and ACH uses the CH sound described in the pronunciation chapter.

VEB-SHEM YAG-ALP-ZAK

VEB is *web* with a *v*. SHEM is like *gem* but with a *sh* instead of a *g*. YAG is *bag* with a *y*. ALP is like *scalp* without the *sc*. ZAK is like *back* with a *z* instead of a *b*.

SHER-TATS-LEE-ACH

SHER is like *shirt*, without the *t*. TATS is like *cats* but with a *t* instead of a *c*. LEE is like *leap* without the *p*.

BUR-CAM-EE-AH ZEH

BUR is like the first part of *burden*. CAM is like the first part of *camera*. EE is *bee* without the *b*. AH is the same as the English *ah*. ZEH is like *yeah* but starting with a *z* instead of a *y*.

The individual words of power and angelic names are as follows:

CRASTAN
CRAS is like *crass*, and TAN is like *tan*.

SHAM-SHE-ELL
SHAM is like the first part of *shambles*. SHE is just *she*. ELL is *bell* without the *b*

BAG-EE-TATZ
BAG is *bag*. EE is like *see* without the *s*. TATZ sounds like the English **rats** but with a *t* instead of an *r*, and the *s* extended into a slight *z* sound.

YO-FEE-ELL
YO is like *no* with a *y* instead of an *n*. FEE is like *feel* without the *l*. ELL has been covered.

BUH-TAR TZA-TAG
BUH is like *bug* without the *g*, and the *uh* sound is slightly extended. TAR is *tar*. TZA rhymes with *star*. You make a quick *ts* sound (like the end of *cats*) before ZAR, which is just *car* with a *z* instead of a *c*. TAG is just *tag*.

RACH-ME-ELL
RACH is like *rack*, but with the CH sound already discussed. ME is *me,* and ELL has been covered.

SHUH-KAV TZUH-YAT
SHUH is like the first part of *should*. KAV is like *have* with a *k*. For TZUH make a *t* sound, followed by ZUH, which is like *bug* but starting with a *z* and without the *g*. YAT is like *bat* with a *y* instead of a *b*.

CARVE-EE-ELL

CARVE is *carve*, and the other sounds have been covered.

OAR-PA-KNEE-ELL

OAR is *oar*, PA is *pa*, KNEE is *knee* and ELL has been covered.

NUH-GAD EE-CHASH

NUH is like *bug*, with an *n* instead of a *b*, and without the *g*. GAD is *bad* with *g*. EE has been covered, and CHASH starts with the CH sound followed by *ash*.

KAV-SHE-ELL

KAV is like *have* with a *k*. SHE is *she*. ELL has been covered.

EE-GAL-PUH-ZAK

EE has been covered. GAL is *pal* with a *g*. PUH is *pump* before you get to the *m*. ZAK is like *back* with a *z* instead of a *b*.

LA-HA-VEE-ELL

LA is like *lark* without the *rk*. Ha is *ha*. VEE is like the letter *v*. ELL has been covered.

When Magick Works

The magick in this book works easily for most people, but if you find it difficult, *The Gallery of Magick* website blog contains many FAQs, along with advice and practical information that is updated on a regular basis.

www.galleryofmagick.com

If you have questions, our website is an excellent source of background material and practical posts that help you to get magick working. We could have published two or three books on magickal practice, but instead, it's all there for free. You can also find extensive FAQs for every book. I urge you to make good use of the site when you encounter problems, and also when you wish to expand your understanding of magick.

The Gallery of Magick Facebook page will also keep you up to date. Please note that we only have one official Facebook page, and information in various fan groups is not always accurate.

If you have an interest in developing your magick further, there are many texts that can assist you. *The Angels of Alchemy* works with 42 angels, to obtain personal transformation. *The 72 Sigils of Power*, by Zanna Blaise, covers Contemplation Magic (for insight and wisdom) and Results Magic (for changing the world around you). Zanna is also the author of *The Angels of Love*, which uses a tasking method with six angels to heal relationships or to attract a soulmate.

The 72 Angels of Magick explores hundreds of powers that can be applied by working with these angels. *Words of Power* and *The Greater Words of Power* present an extremely simple ritual practice, for bringing about change in yourself and others, as well as directing and attracting changed circumstances.

For those seeking more money, *Magickal Cashbook* uses a ritual to attract small bursts of money out of the blue, and works best when you are not desperate, but when you can approach the magick with a sense of enjoyment and pleasure. *Magickal Riches* is more comprehensive, with rituals for everything from gambling to sales. There is also a master ritual to oversee magickal income. For the more ambitious, *Wealth Magick* contains a complex set of rituals for earning money by building a career. For those still trying to find their feet, there is *The Magickal Job Seeker.*

For those who cannot find peace through protection, there is *Magickal Attack*, by Gordon Winterfield. Dark magick is not to everybody's taste, but this is a highly moral approach that puts the emphasis on using authority to restore peace.

Magickal Seduction is a text that looks at attracting others by using magick to amplify your attractive qualities, rather than through deception. *Adventures in Sex Magick* is a more specialized text, for those open-minded enough to explore this somewhat extreme form of magick.

The Master Works of Chaos Magick by Adam Blackthorne is an overview of self-directed and creative magick, which also includes a section covering the Olympic Spirits. *Magickal Servitors* takes another aspect of Chaos Magick and updates it into a modern, workable method.

Sigils of Power and Transformation, by Adam Blackthorne, presents a unique magickal method and is our most popular and effective magick to date. *Archangels of Magick* by Damon Brand is the most complete book of magick we have published, covering sigils, divination, invocation, and evocation.

Damon Brand

www.galleryofmagick.com

Made in the USA
Columbia, SC
17 September 2023

22992747R00059